CORAL REEFS

of the Caribbean, The Bahamas and Florida

Alfonso Silva Lee and Roger E. Dooley

CARIBBEAN

First published 1998 by
MACMILLAN EDUCATION LTD
London and Basingstoke
Companies and representatives throughout the world

ISBN 0–333–67402–2

10 9 8 7 6 5 4 3 2 1
07 06 05 04 03 02 01 00 99 98

This book is printed on paper suitable for recycling and
made from fully managed and sustained forest sources.

Typeset by EXPO Holdings, Malaysia

Printed in Hong Kong

A catalogue record for this book is available from the
British Library.

Illustrations by Román Compañy (pp. 5, 22–59, 64–67, 72–75), Rafael Cordovés (pp. 6–21) and
Rodolfo Peña Mora (pp. 60–63, 68–71)

Cover illustration by Román Compañy

ACKNOWLEDGEMENTS
Darío Guitart, C. Lavett Smith, Pedro Alcolado and Nereida Martinez critically read the
manuscript, and their comments allowed its transformation into the mature and final version.
Román Compañy, Rafael Cordovés and Rodolfo Peña all deserve the greatest appreciation for
their patience and skill in the accurate, proficient and time-consuming task of producing the
excellent drawings.

CONTENTS

INTRODUCTION

Lakes, cliffs, mountains and estuaries undoubtedly make the heart beat faster, inspire meditation, spark happiness. But of all natural environments, coral reefs are – no question about this – the most spectacular. Animal life here comes in exuberant colours, forms and behaviours: an incredible visual carnival.

The warm waters of the Caribbean, the Bahamas and the neighbouring continental shelf are crowded with coral reefs. Some grow so close to the coast that you can dive into them from the shore. Others form barriers that skirt the coast for miles. Still other reefs are hidden deeper into the ocean – 60 or more feet under the surface – typically where the seabed has sudden vertical faults, with caverns, crags and promontories that mark ancient coastlines formed 17 000 and 35 000 years back, when dozens of metres of water were stolen from the ocean by the frigid planet. Today that liquid has returned to its enormous container, and the quiet darkish blue waters teem with corals as fragile as porcelain, soft-tissued sponges up to two metres long, iridescent yellow fish, and the highly prized black coral.

The coral reef's only drawback is its fragility. Reefs are geologically ancient ecosystems evolved in conditions of extreme stability. As a result, large numbers of species have established tight interrelationships. There are worms adapted to live inside the grooves of sponges; fish and shrimp painted like clowns, committed to cleaning parasites off the skin, mouths and gills of a multifarious reef population; hermit crabs that befriend anemones for a better defence against octopuses; crabs that live hidden in small crevices of living coral; and near-blind shrimp that depend on the quick reactions of tiny fish to warn them of approaching dangers. Another association, this one between corals and single-celled algae, is so close and widespread that the entire reef's existence depends on it.

- This guide includes 337 species of the largest, most common, visible and colourful animals and plants of the Western North Atlantic and Caribbean reefs.

- Maximum size is shown in brackets after each species' description. Specimens observed underwater will probably appear much smaller.

- In some species males and females differ in appearance. They are identified in illustrations by the symbols ♂ and ♀ respectively. Juveniles are designated by the abbreviation '**juv**'.

- Some species of invertebrates and plants are hard to tell apart at a glance. In such cases only the genus is given, followed by the abbreviation spp, for 'species'.

- Animals which are considered in any way dangerous are labelled by showing their common names in ***bold italic type***. The text explains why they are potentially hazardous.

SHARKS AND RAYS

These are special kinds of fish, whose skeletons – made of cartilage instead of bone – are very light and flexible. They have been around for a very long time – 400 million years – testifying to the efficiency of the original design for the task of collecting meat. Evolution has endowed most of the 780 species – 380 of sharks and 400 of rays – with keen senses of smell, taste and hearing. Another sense picks up weak electric fields generated by prey; two additional sense organs have functions which are still unknown.

Both sharks and rays are strict carnivores. Sharks generally depend on their speed to reach their elusive prey, and on slashing teeth and strength to overcome them. Rays are serene animals, specialised in feeding on extremely small or highly armoured animals, or in hunting with unconventional tactics.

Rays are quite friendly. None of the species considers humans as potential prey. Some species of sharks, however, are capable of making that unfortunate connection. Blood attracts sharks and intense, erratic movements may trigger an attack. The risk of an assault is nevertheless very remote and the sudden appearance of a shark should not be cause for panic. Although only a small portion of their bad reputation is well deserved, it is always advisable to leave the water as calmly as possible.

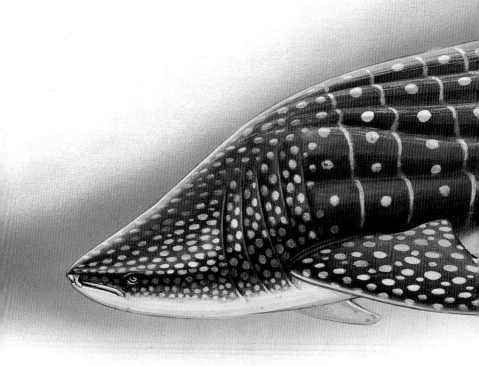

1 Whale shark

Rhincodon typus
Holds the record for the largest fish in
the world. A veritable monster, but
slow and harmless. Feeds on animal
plankton and small fish. Rarely found
near reefs. If you are lucky enough to
see one, get closer for a better look:
you will remember the moment for the
rest of your life. (60 ft.)

2 Nurse shark

Ginglymostoma cirratum
Nocturnal. Spends the day resting motionless on the sea floor. Feeds on crustaceans and fish. Harmless, but may bite if provoked. Teeth are small, but they hold on tenaciously, and the result may be fatal. (14 ft.)

3 Tiger shark

Galeocerdo cuvieri
Very dangerous. Has attacked humans, sometimes with fatal consequences. Feeds on all kinds of marine animals, particularly turtles. (24 ft.)

4 Lemon shark

Negaprion brevirostris
Common near reefs, even in shallow water. Feeds on rays, trunkfish, crustaceans, octopuses and seabirds. Bears a litter of 5–17 young. May attack humans. (11 ft.)

5 Great hammerhead

Sphyrna mokarran
Very dangerous and diabolical-looking. Frequents the open sea. Various hypotheses attempt to explain the function of such an oddly-shaped head: improved manoeuvrability, a greater perception of odour directionality, and the ability to track down prey buried in the sand by homing in on their electrical fields. (20 ft.)

6 Reef shark

Carcharhinus perezi
Common in coastal waters. Considered dangerous, like the other species of the same genus. (9.8 ft.)

7 Blacktip shark

Carcharhinus limbatus
Primarily an open water shark, but may approach reefs in pursuit of schooling fish. (8.2 ft.)

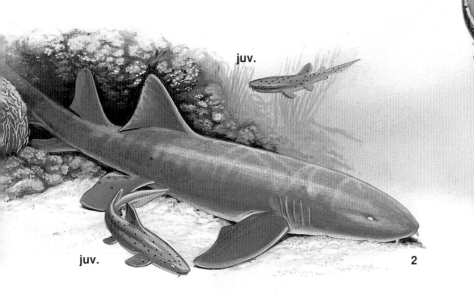

juv.

juv.

2

3

4

5

6

7

9

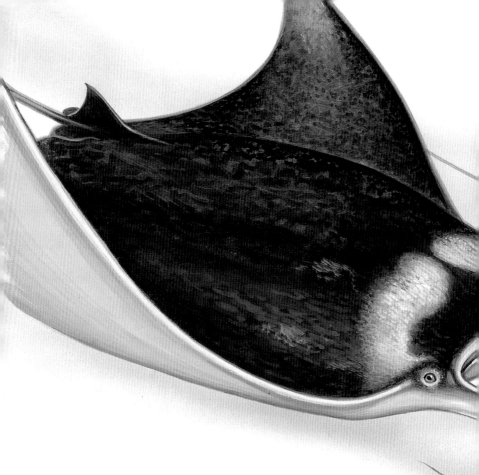

8 Atlantic manta
Manta birostris
A huge but harmless giant. The 'horns'
which give it such an aggressive
appearance are soft skin folds that
help form a funnel for capturing animal
plankton. (22 ft. wide)

9 Spotted eagle ray
Aetobatus narinari
Impressive. Sails over the reef like a
huge bird. Feeds on molluscs, which
are crushed in the throat with
formidable strength. Never attacks
humans. Has five defensive spines at
the base of the tail. (8 ft. wide)

10 Southern stingray
Dasyatis americana
Generally seen by day lying immobile
on the sand or slightly buried in it.
Never attacks humans, but if provoked
or frightened, it may sting with the long
poison-loaded spine at the base of the
tail. (6 ft. wide)

11 Yellow-spotted stingray
Urolophus jamaicensis
Common. A spine containing a painful
venom lies over the tail. Does not
usually bury itself in the sand, and is
therefore easy to spot and avoid.
Feeds at night. (14 in. wide)

9

8

10

11

11

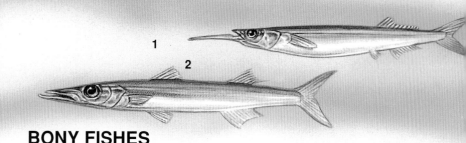

BONY FISHES

About 600 species of scaly creatures enliven and brighten the Caribbean reef scenery. Two hundred and two are included here. With a wide range of feeding habits, they include super-heavyweights and under-one-inch dwarfs; solitary landlords and silvery slaves of life among the crowd; grey sentinels of the night and light-loving clowns. Of ancient lineage, their lives are now entwined with the reef: the coral environment provides the means of defence, reproduction, rest and sleep.

To satisfy their appetites they use the most varied and subtle tactics, only apparently infallible. Mouths have been transformed into specialised feeding instruments: long tubes for suctioning from a distance, delicate pincers, toothed nippers, pruning knives, crunchers, or enormous toothless funnels with an astonishing capacity for removing from the scene, in an instant, heavy and spiny prey.

1 Ballyhoo
Hemiramphus brasiliensis
Feeds on floating or drifting seagrasses and tiny fish. May flee along the surface propelling itself with the lower lobe of its tail fin. (16 in.)

2 Southern sennet
Sphyraena picudilla
Nocturnal. Swims during the day in schools of up to hundreds of individuals. (18 in.)

3 Dwarf herring
Jenkinsia lamprotaenia
Forms school of tens of thousands at the entrance of caves or protected coastal shallows. At night they disperse in search of plankton. (3 in.)

4 Redfin needlefish
Strongylura notata
A diurnal predator. Inhabits only the top few feet of coastal waters. The long mouth is armed with dozens of long, pointed teeth. (2 ft.)

3

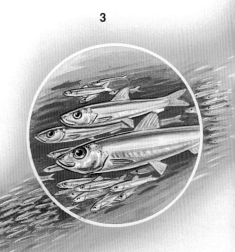

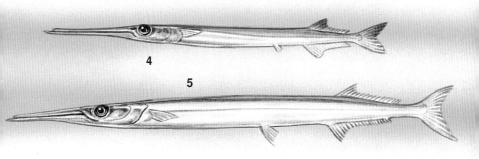

5 Houndfish

Tylosurus crocodilus
A swift hunter. Catches prey both by swimming and leaping through the air. (5 ft.)

6 Tarpon

Megalops atlanticus
Bathed in silver, and gregarious. Usually found in estuaries and bays, but also frequents the reefs. Nocturnal. Feeds on small shrimp and fish just below the surface of the water. (8 ft.)

7 Snook

Centropomus undecimalis
Eats both fish and crabs with its enormous mouth. Lives only on reefs growing near estuaries and mangrove swamps. (4 ft.)

8 Great barracuda

Sphyraena barracuda
A predator with large, sharp teeth; common and generally solitary. Most active at dawn and dusk. May approach divers out of curiosity, but is harmless if not provoked. The flesh can be toxic. (6.5 ft.)

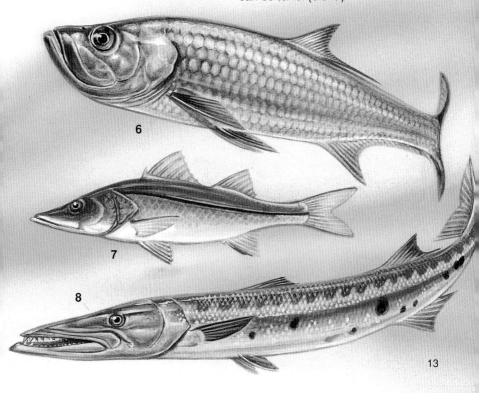

9 Trumpetfish
Aulostomus maculatus
Hides among soft coral branches, often in a vertical position, head down, stalking small fish. A complex mouth apparatus allows the sucking in of prey from several inches away. (3 ft.)

10 Green moray
Gymnothorax funebris
Common. Hides in dark caves and emerges to eat only at night. Will bite any intruder in its territory swiftly and powerfully. (8 ft.)

11 Goldentail moray
Muraena miliaris
Very beautiful and tranquil. This last trait, along with its small size, make it hard to find. (2 ft.)

12 Spotted moray
Gymnothorax moringa
Common and nocturnal. Has a keen sense of smell. Feeds on fish tracked down by following their scent. May bite if provoked. (3 ft.)

13 Garden eel
Heteroconger halis
Found on sandy bottoms in colonies numbering up to hundreds. Never leaves its hole entirely. Feeds during the day on animal plankton swept in by the current, and in doing so sways its body gracefully. (20 in.)

14 Sand diver
Synodus intermedius
Solitary and never abundant. Hunts both day and night, lying in ambush on the bottom, either among rocks or partially buried in the sand. (18 in.)

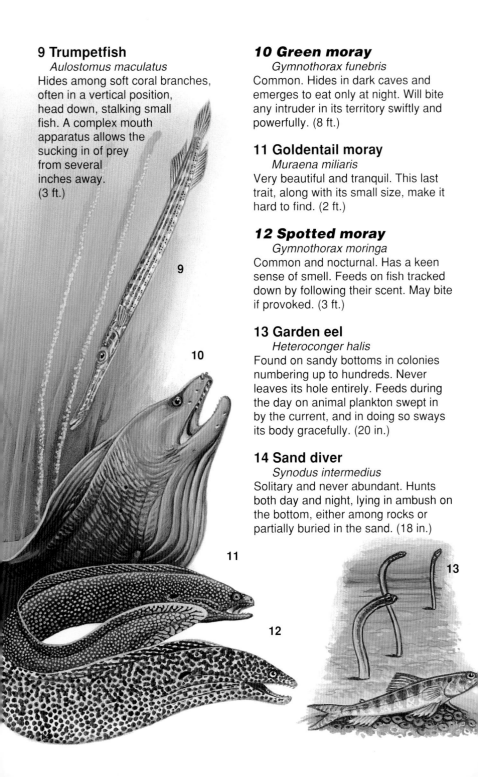

15 Yellow goatfish
Mulloidichthys martinicus
Gregarious and usually nocturnal. Frequents sandy bottoms and uses its long whiskers to probe the sediment in search of buried invertebrates. (15 in.)

16 Spotted goatfish
Pseudupeneus maculatus
Solitary and diurnal. (1 ft.)

17 Blue-spotted cornetfish
Fistularia tabacaria
A predator inhabiting turtle grass-covered seabeds that surround reefs. (6 ft. excluding tail filament)

18 High-hat
Equetus acuminatus
Hides in caves during the day, in groups of up to 20 individuals; at night they disperse in search of shrimp and other invertebrates. (9 in.)

19 Jacknife-fish
Equetus lanceolatus
The rarest species of the genus; lives in deeper reefs. (10 in.)

20 Spotted drum
Equetus punctatus
Solitary. Feeds on small shrimp and crabs. (10 in.)

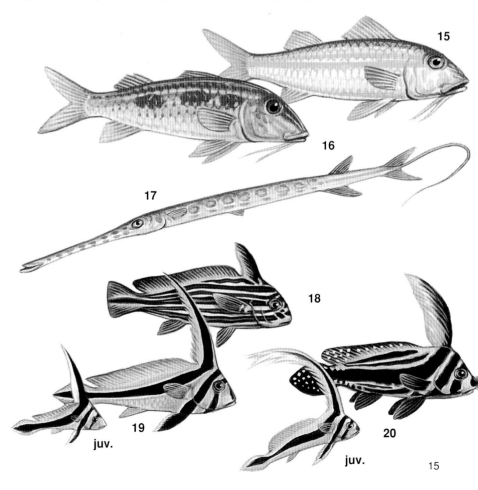

15
16
17
18
19 juv.
20
juv.

SOLDIERFISH AND SQUIRRELFISH

All are nocturnal and pursue their prey – crabs, shrimp and molluscs – mainly by sight. During the day they seek shelter among the corals. Some species are very territorial and use their gas bladders to produce intimidating, drum-like beats. The squirrelfishs' long spine on the gill cover contains poison; its jab is quite painful, but otherwise not seriously harmful.

1 Blackbar soldierfish
Myrypristis jacobus
Spends the day in large caves in groups of up to 100 individuals. Feeds on animal plankton. (8 in.)

2 Longjaw squirrelfish
Holocentrus marianus (6.5 in.)

3 Longspine squirrelfish
Holocentrus rufus (10 in.)

4 Squirrelfish
Holocentrus adscensionis (1 ft.)

5 Reef squirrelfish
Holocentrus coruscus (4 in.)

6 Dusky squirrelfish
Holocentrus vexillarius (7 in.)

BIGEYES AND SWEEPER

7 Bigeye
Priacanthus arenatus
Found in somewhat deeper water. Small groups can be seen by day in places exposed to sunlight. (1 ft.)

8 Glasseye snapper
Priacanthus cruentatus
Solitary. Hides in dark caves during the day. At night feeds on animal plankton (fish, shrimp and crab larvae). (15 in.)

9 Glassy sweeper
Pempheris schomburgki
Feeds on animal plankton at night. By day congregates in dense schools within large caves. (5 in.)

SOAPFISHES

10 Spotted soapfish
Rypticus subbifrenatus
Seldom seen during the day. (7 in.)

11 Greater soapfish
Rypticus saponaceus
Solitary. Prefers rugged bottoms with plenty of nooks and crannies. Carnivorous and nocturnal. The skin glands secrete strong toxins; has never been found in the stomach of any predator. (13 in.)

7

8

9

10

11

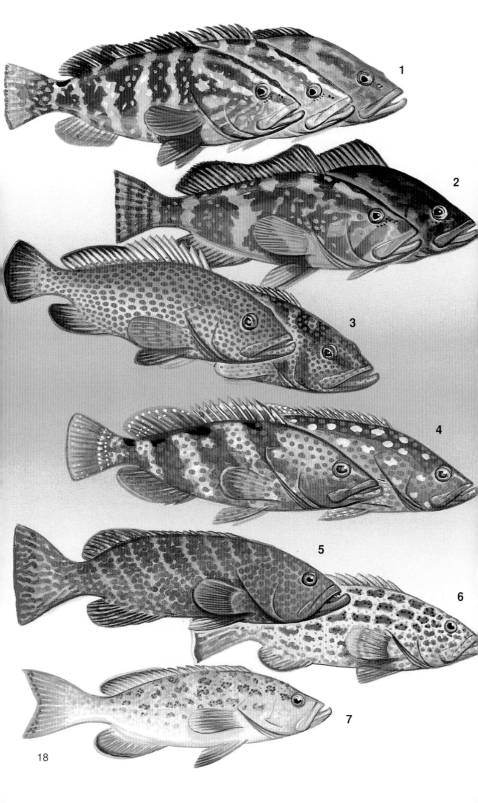

GROUPERS

With immense mouths and totally indiscrimate palates, they are the quintessential predators of the coral world.

Like chameleons, they change colour to blend in with their surroundings, growing lighter or darker in a matter of seconds. Some species can also become chequered, striped, polka-dotted or blushed. Individual fish always begin adult life as females and change sex after several years. Their unspecialised nature allows them to be active round-the-clock, with activity increased at dawn and dusk.

The flesh of the species belonging to the genus *Mycteroperca* may be toxic to eat, causing the famous ciguatera poisoning.

1 Nassau grouper
Epinephelus striatus
Common. Keeps close to a rocky shelter. Spawns during the winter, gathering in schools of hundreds. (3 ft.)

2 Red grouper
Epinephelus morio
Rare in the Antilles, but common along the continental coast. (3.5 ft.)

3 Red hind
Epinephelus guttatus (2 ft.)

4 Rock hind
Epinephelus adscensionis (2 ft.)

5 Tiger grouper
Mycteroperca tigris (40 in.)
This and the following species of the genus feed exclusively on a wide variety of fish. (4 ft.)

6 Yellowfin grouper
Mycteroperca venenosa (3 ft.)

7 Yellowmouth grouper
Mycteroperca interstitialis (30 in.)

8 Black grouper
Mycteroperca bonaci

8

9 Coney
Epinephelus fulvus
Very common and timid. Yellow individuals are rare and can change to normal colouring in just a few days. (16 in.)

10 Jewfish
Epinephelus itajara
The colossus of reef predators. Indiscriminately devours fish, rays, lobsters and young sea turtles. (8 ft.)

11 Graysby
Epinephelus cruentatus (1 ft.)

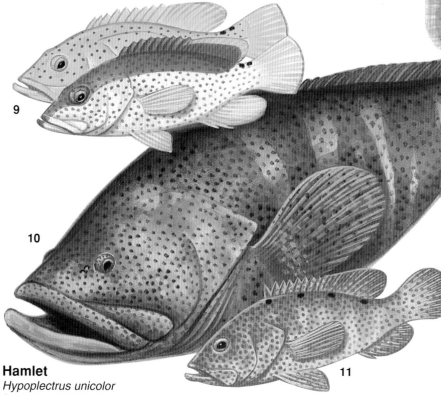

Hamlet
Hypoplectrus unicolor
A master of disguise, has nine known different colour forms, formerly regarded as separate species. A sophisticated undercover predator that tracks down shrimp and crabs in full daylight, using colour patterns that match those of non-predatory fishes, to approach the unsuspecting crustaceans more closely.

A surprising hermaphrodite: every individual is simultaneously male and female. They are capable of fertilising themselves, but generally spawn in pairs, taking turns at different sex roles as they release eggs or sperm.

Each colour form is presented here, with the common and Latin name used in the past. (5 in.)

a Yellowbellied hamlet
Hypoplectrus aberrans
Takes on the colouring of several species of adult damselfish (*Pomacentrus* spp.).

b Blue hamlet
Hypoplectrus gemma
Imitates the Blue chromis.

c Butter hamlet
Hypoplectrus unicolor
Mimics the pattern of the Foureye butterflyfish.

d Black hamlet
Hypoplectrus nigricans
Imitates the Blue tang and/or Black durgon.

e Shy hamlet
Hypoplectrus guttararius
Imitates the Rock beauty.

f Yellowtail hamlet
Hypoplectrus chlorurus
A mimic of the Yellowtail damselfish.

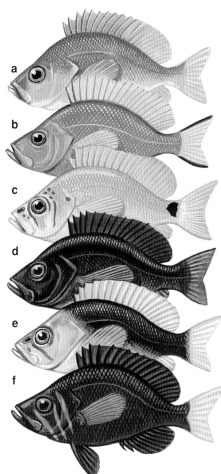

g Golden hamlet
Hypoplectrus gummigutta
May deceive prey by 'impersonating' juvenile Threespot damselfish or Blue tang.

h Indigo hamlet
Hypoplectrus indigo
Possibly a mimic of male Sergeant major when defending its nest.

i Barred hamlet
Hypoplectrus puella
Perhaps a poor – though effective – mime of the Banded butterflyfish?

21

BASSLETS, SEABASSES AND HAWKFISH

1 Tobacco fish
Serranus tabacarius
Found on sandy bottoms near reefs, at depths of between 30 and 100 feet. Feeds on animal plankton. (6 in.)

2 Orangeback bass
Serranus annularis
Abounds only at depths below 80 feet, on flat as well as rough bottoms. (2.5 in.)

3 Lantern bass
Serranus baldwini
Common on sandy bottoms near reefs. When in shallow water (above 40 feet) shows a dull greyish-green coloration. (2 in.)

4 Harlequin bass
Serranus tigrinus
Active during the day. Pairs are easily spotted over sandy patches or among soft corals. Feeds mainly on shrimp. The most common member of this genus. (4 in.)

5 Creole-fish
Paranthias furcifer
Lives below 30 feet, forming loose schools that rise several feet above the bottom in search of planktonic crustaceans. When in danger they dive into the reef and hide. (15 in.)

6 Redspotted hawkfish
Amblycirrhitus pinos
Solitary. Usually lies quietly on the bottom, and therefore is not easy to spot. Feeds on animal plankton, always near the bottom. (3 in.)

7 Royal gramma
Gramma loreto
Very abundant, typical of vertical faults or steep bottoms and large caves (occupying the ceiling and walls). Does not wander more than a couple of feet from these surfaces and flees into narrow holes at the slightest sign of danger. Feeds on animal plankton. Incubates eggs in its mouth. (3 in.)

8 Blackcap basslet
Gramma melacara
Perhaps the most elegant fish of the Caribbean: colour, body shape and movements all contribute. Habits are similar to those of the Royal gramma, but frequents greater depths. (4 in.)

9 Candy basslet
Liopropoma carmabi
Lives below 100 feet, deeper than the Peppermint bass, and in more exposed environments. (2 in.)

10 Peppermint bass
Liopropoma rubre
Although diurnal, lives permanently in the shadows, deep inside dark coral galleries. Carnivorous, solitary and very handsome, but rare and shy. (3.5 in.)

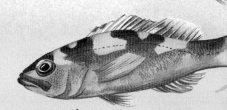

2

1

JACKS

Shiny silvery torpedos, diurnal and carnivorous, they specialise in the pursuit and capture of tiny fish. Groups rarely exceed the few dozens and are not particular to any part of the reef. They travel freely over wide areas, although they may cover the same ground day after day.

1 Yellow jack
Caranx bartholomaei
They attack large schools of herring in groups of up to 10 individuals. When they cruise over the reef every small fish flees for cover. (40 in.)

2 Bar jack
Caranx ruber
Common. Juveniles, in groups of 20–30, feed on surface plankton. Solitary adults or small schools patrol the reef close to the bottom, feeding on almost any kind of fish. (2 ft.)

3 Crevalle jack
Caranx hippos
Adults tend to be solitary. Although rare, they can be found in schools of up to 100. The flesh may cause ciguatera poisoning. (4 ft.)

4 Horse-eye jack
Caranx latus
Gregarious. Feeds almost exclusively on fish. The large eyes indicate nocturnal habits. May cause ciguatera poisoning. (30 in.)

5 Blue runner
Caranx crysos
Lives in open waters, but occasionally raids the reef. Forms large schools. (20 in.)

6 Black jack
Caranx lugubris
Rare and usually solitary or in pairs. Inhabits waters below 80 feet. Eating the flesh may cause ciguatera poisoning. (40 in.)

7 African pompano
Alectis ciliaris
Found in deep water, usually in small groups. (42 in.)

8 Greater amberjack
Seriola dumerili
Inhabits open waters but frequents the reefs. A well-known cause of ciguatera poisoning. (5 ft.)

9 Permit
Trachinotus falcatus
Rare. May live alone or in small groups, both over offshore reefs and in very shallow water. Feeds on many kinds of invertebrates: molluscs, sea urchins, hermit crabs, worms. (45 in.)

10 Florida pompano
Trachinotus carolinus
Coastal. Also penetrates inlets and mangrove shores. (25 in.)

11 Palometa
Trachinotus goodei
Small schools patrol clear beach waters. (20 in.)

MACKEREL, TUNNY AND COBIA

1 Spanish mackerel
Scomberomorus maculatus
The smallest of three tireless and voracious fish eaters. Gregarious. Prefers the coast. (33 in.)

2 Cero
Scomberomorus regalis
Generally solitary. May leap 10–15 feet through the air to land precisely and prey on a school of fish. (34 in.)

3 King mackerel
Scomberomorus cavalla
Somewhat solitary; found in deep reefs. The flesh may cause ciguatera poisoning. (5.5 ft.)

4 Cobia
Rachycentron canadum
Devourer of crabs and shrimp, as well as armoured fish, such as trunkfish. Rarely found on the reefs. (6 ft.)

5 Little tunny
Euthynnus alletteratus
Crosses the reefs at great speed in tight schools. Feeds on small ocean fish and squid. (3.2 ft.)

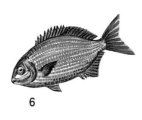

5

CHUB AND REMORAS

6 Bermuda chub
Kyphosus sectatrix
Diurnal and spirited, feeds on many kinds of algae. Travels in small groups. (14 in.)

6

7 Sharksucker
Echeneis naucrates
Free rider thanks to a simple and efficient sucker, used to hang on to sharks, rays, fish or turtles. Feeds on animal plankton as well as leftovers or parasites from its host. (3 ft.)

8 Remora
Remora remora
Inhabits open waters and is a common traveller on the backs of great oceanic sharks. (30 in.)

7

8

SNAPPERS

An abundant and successful group of reef species. All are carnivorous and represent a moderate compromise between the swift and sharp-toothed mackerels and the sluggish, big-mouthed groupers. Some species form schools of dozens to thousands during the day; they seem active, but are really resting. At night they disperse and can travel considerable distances to vast fields of turtlegrass in search of food.

1 Mutton snapper
Lutjanus analis
The low-set mouth and high-placed eyes brand this species as a digger. Seeks prey – crabs, hermits and molluscs – on sandy bottoms, and is skilled at unearthing quarry hidden in the sediment. Also consumes fish. (30 in.)

2 Lane snapper
Lutjanus synagris
The most gregarious of the group. Prefers grassy bottoms, where it forms schools of up to thousands of individuals. (14 in.)

3 Gray snapper
Lutjanus griseus
Common on the reef and in the mangrove belt. Easily moves into fresh water. Juveniles feed mainly on crustaceans, while adults prefer fish. (2 ft.)

4 Schoolmaster
Lutjanus apodus
The commonest of snappers and the most seasoned in swimming through tight and intricate caves. (2 ft.)

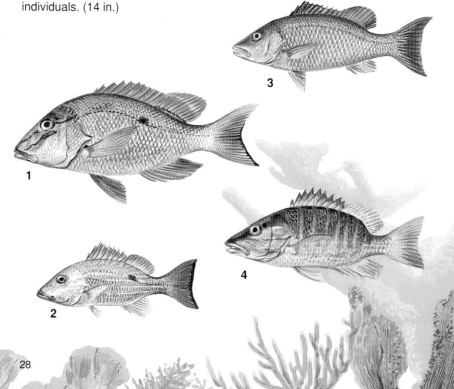

5 Mahogony snapper
Lutjanus mahogony
Forms large schools that remain organised and calm throughout the day. The large eyes testify to strictly nocturnal habits. (15 in.)

6 Dog snapper
Lutjanus jocu
Archetypal reef predator; remains on guard 24 hours a day. Consumes a wide variety of coral fishes. (3 ft.)

7 Cubera snapper
Lutjanus cyanopterus
Small groups of these grey giants swim freely over the reefs. Mostly fish-eaters, although lobsters and large crabs are also devoured. (5 ft.)

8 Yellowtail snapper
Ocyurus chrysurus
Very abundant. Loose schools rise well above the substrate in search of animal plankton. Diurnal as well as nocturnal. (30 in.)

5

6

7

8

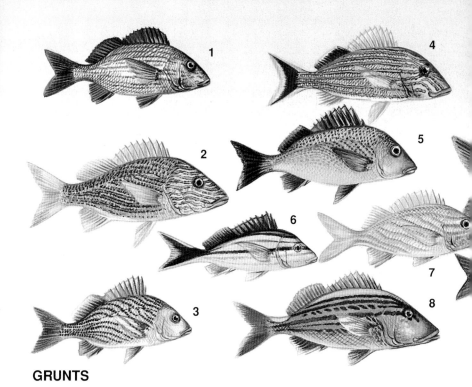

GRUNTS

The most abundant fishes in some Atlantic reefs, grunts are as a rule gregarious, nocturnal and carnivorous. Underwater it is possible to hear the characteristic sounds which give these fish their common name; they are produced by grinding special teeth in their throats. These sounds serve to intimidate others of their kin in the unending contest for available shelters among the corals. The main function of these teeth, however, is to grind the various invertebrates which constitute their food, among them many protected by hard shells.

1 Caesar grunt
Haemulon carbonarium
Gregarious. Prefers rugged bottoms.
(14 in.)

2 White grunt
Haemulon plumieri
Dwells mainly on flat reefs. Territorial defence is expressed through a sort of 'kiss' between the two rivals. (18 in.)

3 Black grunt
Haemulon bonariense (1 ft.)

4 Bluestriped grunt
Haemulon sciurus
Gregarious at times; territorial at others. Also 'kisses' in defence of territory. (18 in.)

5 Sailors choice
Haemulon parrai
Strictly nocturnal, feeds on shrimp and crabs. (16 in.)

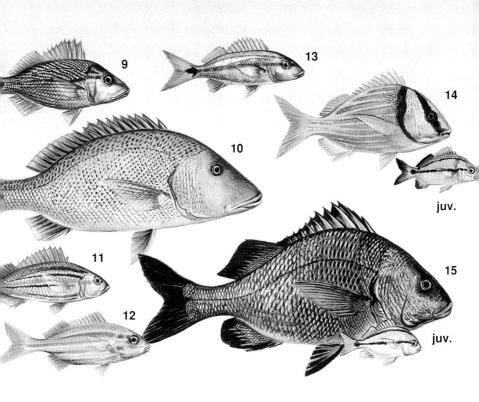

6 Cottonwick
Haemulon melanurum (13 in.)

7 French grunt
Haemulon flavolineatum
Forms schools over the reefs in
shallow waters. (1 ft.)

8 Spanish grunt
Haemulon macrostomum
Nocturnal. Feeds on the apparently
inaccessible black sea urchins. (16 in.)

9 Latin grunt
Haemulon steindachneri (1 ft.)

10 Margate
Haemulon album
Digs in the sand for its assorted prey.
(2 ft.)

11 Striped grunt
Haemulon striatum
Diurnal. Feeds on animal plankton.
(11 in.)

12 Smallmouth grunt
Haemulon chrysargyreum (9 in.)

13 Tomtate
Haemulon aurolineatum (10 in.)

14 Porkfish
Anisotremus virginicus
Juveniles clean parasites off the
bodies of other fish. (15 in.)

15 Black margate
Anisotremus surinamensis
Solitary. Hides in caves during the
day. Lives off assorted sea urchins
and molluscs. (2 ft.)

SPADEFISH, MOJARRAS, TILEFISH AND FLOUNDER

1 Atlantic spadefish
Chaetodipterus faber
Common in groups of several dozen, midway between the bottom and the surface. Diurnal; feeds on sponges, gorgonians, algae, seagrasses, planktonic larvae and sea cucumbers. (3 ft.)

2 Yellowfin mojarra
Gerres cinereus
Diurnal, and possibly nocturnal. Lives on sandy bottoms near reefs. Somewhat solitary. The distinctive mouth protrudes forward and downward, to facilitate in poking the sand or mud for invertebrates. (16 in.)

3 Spotfin mojarra
Eucinostomus argenteus
Solitary and typical of sandy bottoms. Feeds on small invertebrates. (8 in.)

4 Sand tilefish
Malacanthus plumieri
Lives on sandy bottoms among scattered coral fragments; uses these to build a cave, into which it flees head first when in danger. Feeds on brittle starfish, crabs, shrimp. (2 ft.)

5 Peacock flounder
Bothus lunatus
A living proof of animal adaptability and the fantasy of evolution. Lies on its right (white) side, while both eyes are located on the left side. Feeds on fish, crabs and shrimp. (18 in.)

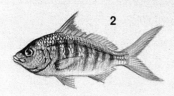

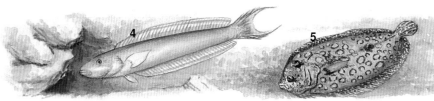

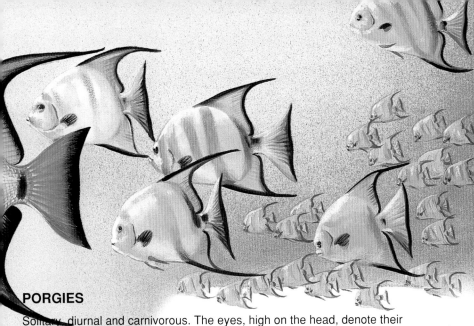

PORGIES

Solitary, diurnal and carnivorous. The eyes, high on the head, denote their nature as diggers. They feed on assorted invertebrates, mostly armoured, grinding the hard shells with powerful molar teeth. They do not seek protection within the coral labyrinths, preferring to keep a prudent distance from sources of potential danger.

6 Saucereye porgy
Calamus calamus (16 in.)

7 Sheepshead porgy
Calamus penna (18 in.)

8 Jolthead porgy
Calamus bajonado (2 ft.)

9 Pluma
Calamus pennatula (15 in.)

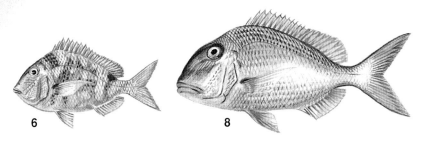

6

8

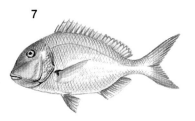

7

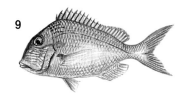

9

BUTTERFLYFISHES AND ANGELFISHES

Like decorated dishes with fins, they are present in every dive and every reef. Always solitary or in pairs, their colouring serves as a flag, ensuring that each species avoids having territorial disputes with others. All are diurnal and, as a rule, very specialised carnivores.

1 Foureye butterflyfish
Chaetodon capistratus
The most common of its genus. Feeds on tentacles torn off small colonial anemones and stationary worms. (3 in.)

2 Banded butterflyfish
Chaetodon striatus (6 in.)

3 Spotfin butterflyfish
Chaetodon ocellatus (8 in.)

4 Reef butterflyfish
Chaetodon sedentarius (3 in.)

5 Longsnout butterflyfish
Chaetodon aouleatus
Lives at depths exceeding 40 feet. The long snout allows for reaching between the spines of sea urchins to feed on their tiny tentacle-like feet. (3 in.)

6 Gray angelfish
Pomacanthus arcuatus
Adults feed on sponges and algae; juveniles on external parasites of larger reef fishes. (14 in.)

7 French angelfish
Pomacanthus paru (1 ft.)

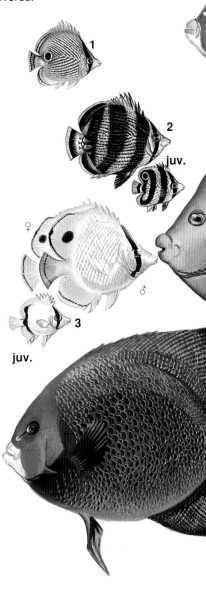

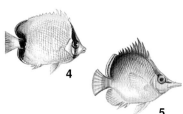

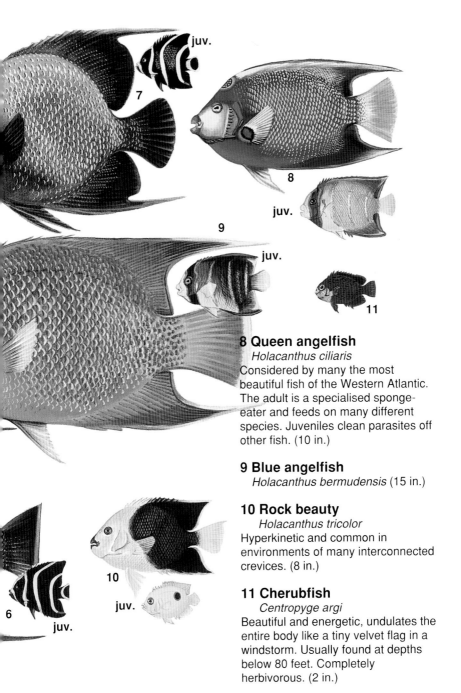

juv.

7

8

juv.

9

juv.

juv.

11

6

juv.

10

juv.

8 Queen angelfish
Holacanthus ciliaris
Considered by many the most
beautiful fish of the Western Atlantic.
The adult is a specialised sponge-
eater and feeds on many different
species. Juveniles clean parasites off
other fish. (10 in.)

9 Blue angelfish
Holacanthus bermudensis (15 in.)

10 Rock beauty
Holacanthus tricolor
Hyperkinetic and common in
environments of many interconnected
crevices. (8 in.)

11 Cherubfish
Centropyge argi
Beautiful and energetic, undulates the
entire body like a tiny velvet flag in a
windstorm. Usually found at depths
below 80 feet. Completely
herbivorous. (2 in.)

1

juv.

2

♂

3

4

juv.

7

juv.

5

juv.

8

6

juv.

9

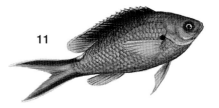

DAMSELFISHES

Small and dynamic. Most species show a similar combination of traits; festive colouring and a rather belligerent nature. Territorial, they inhabit small castles of reef rock and attack most species that dare to come close. Using the tactic of 'nipping the tail area' they are able to fend off even a Great barracuda. Diurnal and mostly omnivorous.

1 Yellowtail damselfish
Microspathodon chrysurus
Strictly herbivorous; feeds on numerous species of delicate algae. Solitary, and fiercely pugnacious. Lives in shallow waters, right up to the shore edge. (8 in.)

2 Sergeant major
Abudefduf saxatilis
Gregarious and diurnal, this species inhabits shallow waters, where it consumes animal plankton – down to the reef, where it devours algae and small invertebrates and seeks protection. Glues eggs to previously cleaned rocky surfaces. The male jealously protects the nest around the clock for 2–3 days. During this time he turns dark blue. (7 in.)

3 Night sergeant
Abudefduf taurus
The largest and most herbivorous of the group. A solitary species that inhabits shallow waters. (10 in.)

4 Dusky damselfish
Pomacentrus fuscus
Omnivorous, solitary and territorial, like the next four species of this genus. (6 in.)

5 Threespot damselfish
Pomacentrus planifrons
Prefers somewhat deeper waters. (5 in.)

6 Beaugregory
Pomacentrus leucostictus
Lives in shallow waters. (4 in.)

7 Cocoa damselfish
Pomacentrus variabilis
Inhabits the deeper waters of the reefs. (5 in.)

8 Honey damselfish
Pomacentrus mellis
Common near the coast, in depths of 5–15 feet. (3 in.)

9 Bicolour damselfish
Pomacentrus partitus
Lives in depths of 15–100 feet. Several individuals inhabit the same coral head, and from there rise a few feet in search of animal plankton. (4 in.)

10 Blue chromis
Chromis cyaneus
Incredibly brightly coloured and beautiful. Gregarious, it feeds on animal plankton like the next species, but in deeper waters and closer to the bottom. (5 in.)

11 Brown chromis
Chromis multilineatus (6.5 in.)

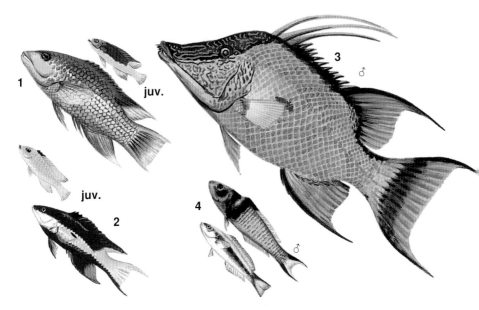

HOGFISHES, WRASSES AND RAZORFISHES

Diurnal and typically solitary, and buck-toothed, for plucking crabs, snails and other invertebrates which inhabit narrow crevices or burrow in the sand.

When swimming placidly they propel themselves by beating the pectoral fins back against the body. Most species never stray more than a few feet above the bottom, and sleep burrowed in the sand.

1 Spanish hogfish
Bodianus rufus
Common in shallow reefs. Constantly in motion; feeds on a large variety of invertebrates: crabs, brittle starfish, sea urchins, molluscs and shrimp. Juveniles pluck parasites off larger fish. (15 in.)

2 Spotfin hogfish
Bodianus pulchellus
Lives in deeper reefs, below 60 feet. (6 in.)

3 Hogfish
Lachnolaimus maximus
Lives on sandy or grassy flats, but can also be found on reefs. Preys on almost one hundred different species of molluscs. (3 ft.)

4 Bluehead
Thallasoma bifasciatum
Abundant right from the shore. The smaller, yellow individuals may be male or female; the larger blueheads are called 'supermales'. The first group spawn in a crowd, while supermales always mate with one female at a time. (7 in.)

5 Slippery dick
Halichoeres bivittatus (8 in.)

6 Puddingwife
Halichoeres radiatus (20 in.)

7 Clown wrasse
Halichoeres maculipinna (7 in.)

8 Yellowhead wrasse
Halichoeres garnoti (7 in.)

9 Creole wrasse
Clepticus parrai
Truly gregarious, and the only 'high-flying' wrasse: rises 30 or more feet from the bottom in search of copepods and other planktonic animals. (1 ft.)

10 Pearly Razorfish
Hemipteronotus novacula
Lives exclusively on sandy bottoms; hides at the slightest sign of danger by diving head first into the sand. Feeds mainly on tiny molluscs. (15 in.)

11 Green Razorfish
Hemipteronotus splendens
Lives on animal plankton, but without rising far above the seabed. Also dives into sand for protection. (6 in.)

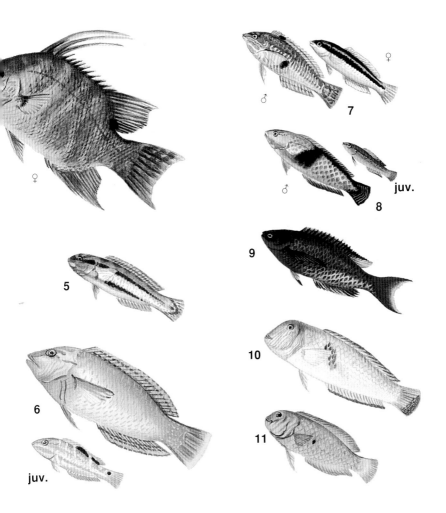

1

2

3

4

5

6

7

8 ♂

8 ♀

PARROTFISHES

Rioting colours and beaks make their common name inevitable. Diurnal, they scrape algae of many different species from the bottom. Each mouthful is ground in the throat with strong teeth; rock scrapings are swallowed along with the algae to assist in this, the plant cells thus surrendering their nutrients. In this manner they 'manufacture' a good portion of the sand present in every reef.

Males and females have very different colouring. More- or less-coloured males of each species spawn, respectively, in pairs or groups.

1 Stoplight parrotfish
Sparisoma viride (20 in.)

2 Striped parrotfish
Scarus croicensis
The most common of the group. May form very large schools. Like several other parrotfish species, at night it secretes a thin, transparent mucous sack that wraps the entire fish, which retains odours that would otherwise attract predators. (11 in.)

3 Redfin parrotfish
Sparisoma rubripinne (18 in.)

4 Princess parrotfish
Scarus taeniopterus (13 in.)

5 Redtail parrotfish
Sparisoma chrysopterum (18 in.)

6 Midnight parrotfish
Scarus coelestinus
Males and females are identical in appearance. (30 in.)

7 Redband parrotfish
Sparisoma aurofrenatum (11 in.)

8 Queen parrotfish
Scarus vetula
Common in small groups composed of a supermale and a half-dozen females and dull-coloured males. (2 ft.)

9 Blue parrotfish
Scarus coeruleus
Solitary and rare. (4 ft.)

10 Rainbow parrotfish
Scarus guacamaia
Even large adults travel in groups of 10 or more. There are no visible differences between the sexes. They sometimes feed in very shallow water, among breaking waves. (4 ft.)

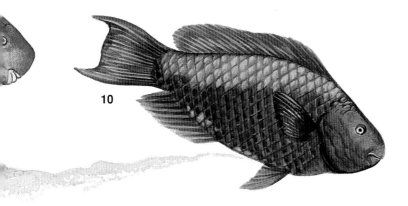

10

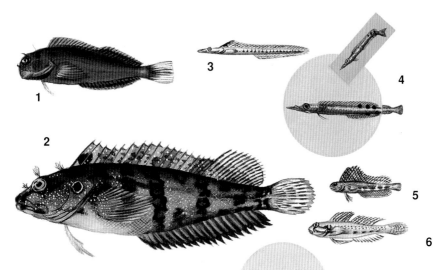

BLENNIES AND GOBIES

1 Redlip blenny
Ophioblennius atlanticus
Herbivorous, territorial and very abundant in shallow reefs. (5 in.)

2 Hairy blenny
Labrisomus nuchipinnis
Solitary; prefers shallow reefs. Diet is composed of crabs, snails, sea urchins, worms and numerous other invertebrates. (9 in.)

3 Yellowface blenny
Chaenopsis limbaughi
Lives in tubular holes inherited from polychaete worms: darts out from there to capture prey. Sometimes two individuals contest the same hole, confronting and butting one another with open mouths. (3.5 in.)

4 Arrow blenny
Lucayablennius zingaro
Possibly the tiniest fish-eating fish of Atlantic reefs. Lives among coral heads, permanently arched and ready to attack. (1.5 in.)

5 Sailfin blenny
Emblemaria pandionis
Stalks animal plankton from a retreat on the bottom. (2 in.)

6 Goldspot goby
Gnatholepis thompsoni
Lives on sandy bottoms and feeds on debris, algae and miniature crustaceans. (3 in.)

7 Masked goby
Coryphopterus personatus
Gregarious. Forms rather loose schools among coral heads. Feeds at night on animal plankton. (1.5 in.)

8 Sponge goby
Gobiosoma horsti
Lives in the main cavity of tubular sponges. Feeds on worm-like parasites which inhabit sponges by the thousands. (2 in.)

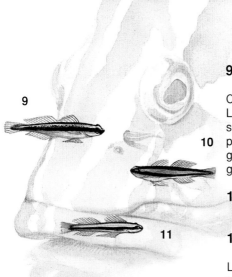

9 Cleaning goby
Gobiosoma genie
Common, and typically found in pairs. Like the following two species it specialises in cleaning external parasites from the body, mouth and gills of larger fish, including morays, groupers and barracudas. (1.7 in.)

10 Neon goby
Gobiosoma oceanops (2 in.)

11 Sharknose goby
Gobiosoma evelynae
Lives at depths below 40 feet, and one to two dozen individuals can converge on a single coral head. (1.5 in.)

JAWFISHES

These are carnivores, diggers, and, with the exception of the charming Yellowhead, nocturnal. All incubate eggs in their mouth.

12 Yellowhead jawfish
Opisthognathus aurifrons (4 in.)

13 Banded jawfish
Opisthognathus macrognathus (8 in.)

14 Mottled jawfish
Opisthognathus maxillosus (5 in.)

TRIGGERFISHES

1 Sargassum triggerfish
Xanthichthys ringens
Common only deeper than 60 feet.
Can form small scattered groups.
Feeds on animal plankton above the
reef. Like the following four species,
the long dorsal spine can be fixed at
will in a raised position, making it more
difficult to swallow. (10 in.)

2 Black durgon
Melichthys niger
Diurnal; inhabits mid-depth reefs.
Feeds on algae, as well as animal
plankton and floating seaweed. Forms
scattered groups of dozens of
individuals. The conspicuous colouring
allows them to see each other from
afar and imitate the flight of the first to
sense danger. (20 in.)

3 Queen triggerfish
Balistes vetula
Diurnal, solitary and common; feeds
primarily on black sea urchins; shells
and spines included! (2 ft.)

4 Ocean triggerfish
Canthidermis sufflamen
Gregarious; generally dwells closer to
the surface than to the seabed. Eats
sea urchins and animal plankton alike.
Swims with a rigid body, flapping the
dorsal and anal fins in an unusual
way. (2 ft.)

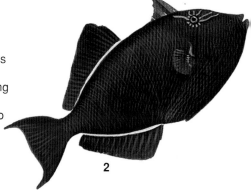

2

3

1

SURGEONFISHES

Diurnal, gregarious and herbivorous; among the most abundant fishes in Western Atlantic reefs. Two of the species have muscular stomachs and ingest much sand, with which algae and seaweed are ground for better digestion. A small, but very sharp, razor-like spine is present on each side of the base of the tail.

5 Blue tang
Acanthurus coeruleus
A common schooling species, and one that swims higher above the bottom. Juveniles may be yellow; these are solitary, territorial, and very aggressive. (9 in.)

6 Doctorfish
Acanthurus chirurgus
Prefers shallow and rather turbid waters. (10 in.)

7 Ocean surgeon
Acanthurus bahianus (1 ft.)

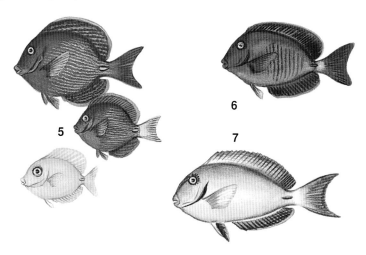

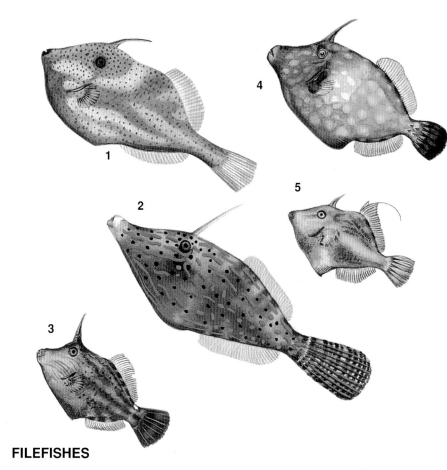

FILEFISHES

1 Orange filefish
Aluterus schoepfi
Solitary or in pairs, inhabits the seabed adjacent to the reefs. They eat exclusively seagrasses and algae. (2 ft.)

2 Scrawled filefish
Aluterus scriptus
A giant if viewed from the side, yet so thin from any other angle as to be almost invisible. Mouth, throat and viscera seem to be armoured: feeds heavily on fire coral and soft coral, totally oblivious to their strong chemicals. (3 ft.)

3 Orangespotted filefish
Cantherhines pullus
The commonest of filefishes. Solitary. Consumes algae, sponges and many other invertebrates. (8 in.)

4 Whitespotted filefish
Cantherhines macrocerus
Rare; generally found in pairs. Feeds on sponges, algae and small invertebrates. (18 in.)

5 Pygmy filefish
Monacanthus setifer (7.5 in.)

TRUNKFISHES AND COWFISHES

Like turtles, their bodies are covered with a hard and rigid case of pure bone; a number of 'windows' allow for eating, seeing and moving the fins. For added protection they also employ toxins, produced by glands in the skin and mouth. In spite of this, many predators devour them. Diurnal and possibly also nocturnal, they are generally solitary, never abundant.

6 Smooth trunkfish
Lactophrys triqueter
Common on the reef. Devours invertebrates which live buried in the sand. (1 ft.)

7 Spotted trunkfish
Lactophrys bicaudalis
Ascidians, sea cucumbers and brittlestars comprise the basis of its diet. (19 in.)

8 Trunkfish
Lactophrys trigonus
Lives in turtlegrass fields; feeds on crabs, molluscs, worms and sea urchins. (18 in.)

9 Scrawled cowfish
Lactophrys quadricornis
Also lives in turtlegrass fields. Feeds on an assortment of bottom-dwelling invertebrates. (19 in.)

10 Honeycomb cowfish
Lactophrys polygonia
Inhabits the reefs and eats soft-shelled invertebrates. (19 in.)

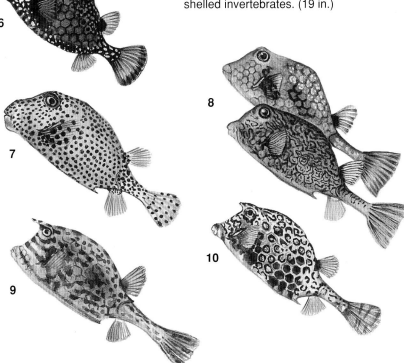

PUFFERS

1 Sharpnose puffer
Canthigaster rostrata
Common below 10–15 feet. Solitary
and aggressive. Frequently seen
chasing one another in defence of
territories. Diurnal, they feed on
seagrasses as well as a wide
selection of invertebrates. (4.5 in.)

2 Bandtail puffer
Sphoeroides spengleri
Capable of puffing up its body with
water, becoming spherical. It is a
mystery how this aids survival. It is a
slow swimmer, with potent toxins in
the liver. Prefers sandy, shallow
environments, feeding on crabs,
molluscs and other invertebrates.
(7 in.)

3 Checkered puffer
Sphoeroides testudineus
Solitary, and common in the shallow
waters surrounding mangrove shores.
(1 ft.)

PORCUPINEFISHES AND BURRFISHES

Capable of puffing up their bodies with water, and for obvious reasons: turned into spiny spheres they present a sound defence. Solitary, at night they seek hard-shelled invertebrates, which they crush with crude, powerful, beak-shaped jaws.

4 Balloonfish
Diodon holacanthus
Rare. Feeds on molluscs, sea urchins and other bottom-dwelling invertebrates. (20 in.)

5 Porcupinefish
Diodon hystrix
Typical of the reef, where it hides in caves during the day. Specialised in crushing the hardest-shelled

Caribbean molluscs with a single bite. (3 ft.)

6 Striped burrfish
Chilomycterus schoepfi (10 in.)

7 Web burrfish
Chilomycterus antillarum
Like the Striped burrfish, it has short, permanently erect spines. (10 in.)

SCORPIONFISHES

Typically motionless, their colour and shape allows them to blend with the rocky seabed, corals and sponges. The dorsal and cheek spines contain a toxin which, although not lethal, can be very painful.

1 Spotted scorpionfish
Scorpaena plumieri
Both diurnal and nocturnal. If disturbed, it displays bold, white-spotted, black patches hidden behind the pectoral fins as a warning to the unwary passer-by. (1 ft.)

2 Reef scorpionfish
Scorpaenodes caribbaeus
Apparently nocturnal; seen by day only rarely. (4 in.)

FROGFISHES AND SARGASSUMFISH

Predators of fish, their success depends on their remarkable camouflage, rock-like immobility, quick-action large mouth, and a tiny 'fishing rod' capable of dangling an attractive 'bait' in front of their mouths. Solitary, diurnal, uncommon and very hard to spot.

3 Spitlure frogfish
Antennarius scaber (6 in.)

5 Longlure frogfish
Antennarius multiocellatus (8 in.)

4 Ocellated frogfish
Antennarius ocellatus (15 in.)

6 Sargassumfish
Histrio histrio (8 in.)

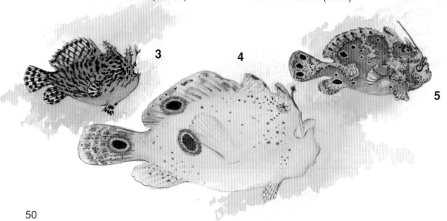

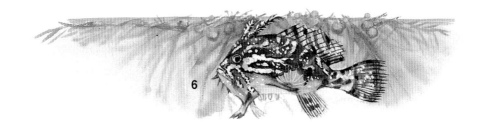

WALKING FISHES

7 Shortnose batfish
Ogcocephalus nasutus
Oddly shaped and rock-like, it lies immobile in ambush for its prey – small fish – in sandy patches. To lure them it hangs a short 'fishing rod with a bait' over its mouth. (15 in.)

8 Lancer dragonet
Callionymus bairdi
Lives on sandy bottoms. May 'walk' with short pelvic fins, or burrow under the sediment. (4 in.)

9 Flying gurnard
Dactylopterus volitans
Does not fly, although its wide fins suggest it might. Heavy and slow; lives on sandy bottoms. May 'walk' with the short lower fins. Extends 'wings' when threatened, possibly to impress would-be predators. Feeds on crustaceans and molluscs. (18 in.)

SPONGES

Having defied, successfully, both common sense and time, sponges are authentic animals, although totally immobile and organless. The most primitive among all multicellular animals, they have survived a thousand and one challenges and catastrophes over a span of 600 million years. More than 300 species inhabit the Caribbean. Their shapes are adapted to the function of filtering water as a means to obtain nourishment: bacteria, debris, dissolved organic matter and planktonic algae. Each species produces a peculiar chemical arsenal for self-defence, and their colours serve the exclusive 'purpose' of announcing their identities to voracious predators: a warning for those considering an easy meal. For us the consequence is a seascape decorated with trumpets, spheres, cups, baskets, networks of rope-like growth, and huge shells of the most elegant shapes, each coloured differently, some with unimaginable pigments.

1 Lavender tube sponge
Spinosella vaginalis
Abundant at depths of 20–30 feet. Commonly has between 5 and 10 tubes, and may be brown, grey, lavender blue, purple or violet; always in pastel tones. (3 ft.)

2 Fire sponge
Tedania ignis
Contact with this species may cause irritation or severe burns. Commonly found in bays and inlets, but also inhabits reefs. (1 ft.)

3 Touch-me-not sponge
Neofibularia nolitangere
May be encrusting or form lobes, always somewhat irregular and thick-walled. Merely brushing against this sponge causes it to secrete toxins that produce irritation and skin sores. (3 ft.)

4 Iridescent tube sponge
Spinosella plicifera
Easy to find and identify. Iridescence may be blue, pink, purple, or even orange. (2.5 ft.)

5 Strawberry sponge
Mycale lavissima
Appears black under water, as the water filters all red components from sunlight. Lives below 30 feet. (1.5 ft.)

1

2

3

6 Basket sponge
Xestospongia muta
Weighs up to 500 lb., and has a hard,
rock-like consistency. (4 ft. wide)

7 Violet tube sponge
Aplysina archeri
Lives in deep waters. Appears violet,
but is truly reddish-brown. Some
colonies are single-tubed, but may
have between 5 and 10. (6 ft.)

8 Yellow tube sponge
Aplysina fistularis
The most spectacular of Caribbean
sponges. At depths below 60 feet it
stands out for its length, geometric
perfection and incredibly brilliant
colour. (6 ft.)

9 Orange ramose sponge
Agelas cilindricus
Common deeper than 60 feet, hanging
from walls and outcrops. May be
8–10 feet long. (branches 1 in. diam.)

CORALS

Corals are unusual animals, capable of forming underwater jungles of pure rock. Each colony comprises between one and several thousand small polyps that typically extend their tentacles only at night. The surface of the hard skeleton has an elaborate embossed design, with ridges and spines, different for each species, where the polyps hide during daylight hours. Within the tissue live unicellular algae in densities of up to 30 000 individuals per cubic millimetre. This association is possibly 150 million years old, one of the oldest mutual aid agreements among organisms. The corals make use of the metabolic riches produced by algae, while the algae are protected by the rocky labyrinth.

1 Staghorn coral
Acropora cervicornis (2 ft.)

2 Elkhorn coral
Acropora palmata
Very abundant at lower depths, where waves break. Swimming among them in rough seas may result in physical injuries. (6 ft.)

3 Club finger coral
Porites porites (1 ft.)

4 Flower coral
Eusmilia fastigiata (2 ft. across)

5 Large flower coral
Mussa angulosa (1.5 ft. across)

6 Pillar coral
Dendrogyra cylindrus (12 ft.)

7 Fused staghorn coral
Acropora prolifera (1 ft.)

55

8 Mountainous star coral
Montastraea annularis
The larger colonies are commonly hollow and provide protection to a large number of fish, crustaceans and molluscs. (6 ft.)

9 Cavernous star coral
Montastraea cavernosa (6 ft.)

10 Mustard hill coral
Porites astreoides
Like many other species of coral, grows in a semi-spherical form only in shallow water. When growing deeper than 50 feet it forms dish-like growths, with the live-side facing up to sunlight. (2 ft.)

11 Green cactus coral
Madracis decactis (1.5 ft.)

12 Rough starlet coral
Siderastraea radians
Wandering colonies up to two inches in diameter can be found in certain sandy environments exposed to the surf. They are totally spherical, with live polyps over the entire surface. (1 ft.)

13 Elliptical star coral
Dichocoenia stokesii (1.5 ft.)

14 Golfball coral
Favia fragum (4 in.)

15 Smooth star coral
Solenastraea bournoni (1.5 ft.)

16 Grooved brain coral
Diploria labyrinthiformis (4 ft. wide)

17 Knobby brain coral
Diploria clivosa (3 ft. wide)

18 Giant brain coral
Colpophyllia natans (4 ft. wide)

19 Smooth brain coral
Diploria strigosa (6 ft. wide)

20 Sinuous cactus coral
Isophyllia sinuosa (8 in.)

21 Butterprint brain coral
Meandrina meandrites (3 ft.)

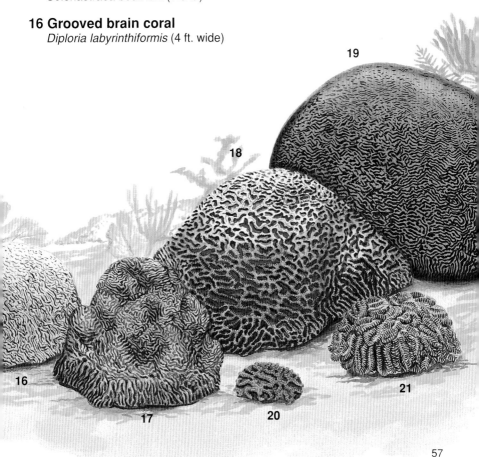

22 Solitary disc coral
Scolymia lacera (6 in. wide)

24 Fungus coral
Mycetophyllia lamarckiana (1 ft.)

23 Leaf coral
Agaricia agaricites (1.5 ft.)

25 Rose coral
Manicina aerolata (6 in.)

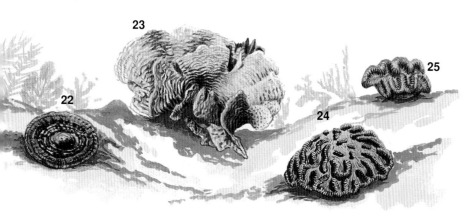

ANEMONES

Cousins of corals, they are generally solitary and have much larger bodies, and are incapable of developing any type of skeleton. They feed on small swimming crustaceans and fish. Prey is captured by means of microscopic poison darts, or by the sticky substance that covers the tentacles. Once trapped, prey is guided to the mouth by the tentacles and swallowed whole. Various species of shrimp live in association with them, totally unharmed.

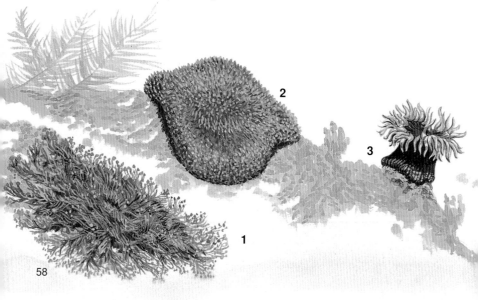

1 Stinging anemone
Lebrunia danae
Generally solitary; lives among live corals, and usually expands the tentacles, covering and killing part of the coral colony's surface. Produces an immediate sharp pain on contact. (1 ft.)

2 Sun anemone
Stoichactis helianthus
Can be very abundant in calm, shallow waters, where they cover parts of the bottom like a carpet. (10 in.)

3 Red warty anemone
Bunodosoma granulifera
Usually found isolated, in shallow waters. (4 in.)

4 Ringed anemone
Bartholomaea annulata
A common retreat for the Arrow crab, the Cardinalfish, and three species of shrimp, one of them tiny, gregarious, orange-striped and planktonic. (1 ft.)

5 Pink-tipped anemone
Condylactis gigantea
Common. Specimens with bright green, instead of pink, tentacle tips are not unusual. (1 ft.)

4

5

GORGONIANS, BLACK CORALS AND FIRE CORALS

Gorgonians and black corals resemble leafless shrubs, oversized feathers, or segments of electric cable. Polyps line the skeleton with a flexible, resistant material they themselves secrete. They feed on microscopic organisms captured with tiny tentacles, and on substances produced by unicellular algae living within their tissues. A multitude of chemical substances are generated to repel would-be predators. Fire corals can be very abundant in shallow reefs at the breakers, and common even at depths of 50 feet.

1 Sea fans
Gorgonia spp.
There are three very similar species. Can be fairly common in reefs in shallow rocky bottoms exposed to ocean waters. (5 ft. wide)

2 Deepwater gorgonian
Iciligorgia schrammi
Found at depths below 60 feet, where water is clean. Grows on reef outcrops, with the concave side facing dominant currents. (6 ft. wide)

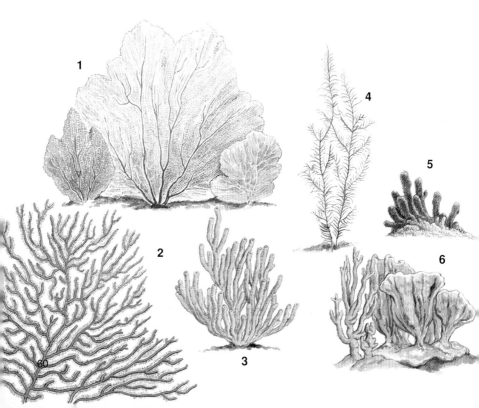

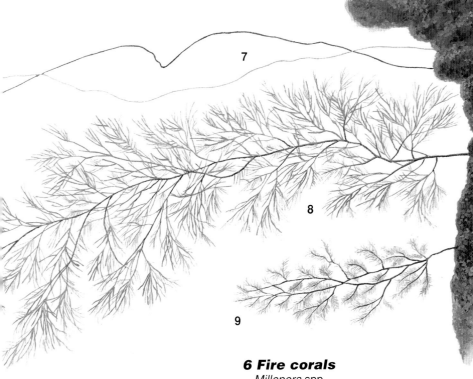

7

8

9

3 Black sea rod
Plexaura homomalla
Abundant in the tranquil waters of reef lagoons; may be recognised by the somewhat flattened branches. Yields substances of wide and important pharmacological use. (3 ft.)

4 Sea plumes
Pseudopterogorgia spp.
Most common at depths of 15–40 feet. Three varieties exist, with colours ranging from whitish through yellow, blue and violet, to purple. (4 ft.)

5 Deadman's fingers
Briareum asbestinum
Lacks a skeleton, and may grow either as thick vertical rods or as an encrusting mat. Very common at shallow depths. (12 in.)

6 Fire corals
Millepora spp.
The several species grow like vertical branches, leafy plates or low encrusting shapes. An instantaneous burning sensation is produced on contact with the skin. (20 in.)

7 Wire coral
Stichopates lutkeni
Sometimes common below 60 feet. Where abundant, gives the deep-reef scenery quite a fanciful and bizarre look. (12 ft.)

8 Black coral
Antipathes salix
Produces the black coral used in jewellery. Colonies are dense and grow in large crevices, caves, or on vertical walls. (12 ft.)

9 Plumed black coral
Antipathes pennacea
Found only at depths below 60 feet. (4 ft.)

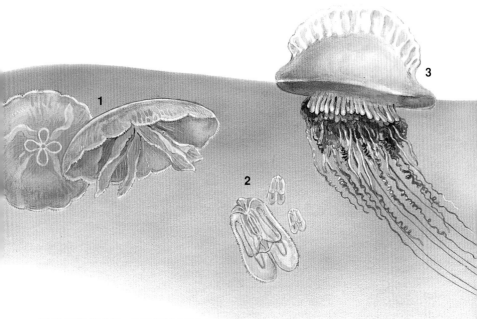

DRIFTING CREATURES

Jellyfish, Portuguese Men-of-war and ctenophores do not belong to the reef, but drift through it. They have jelly-like consistency, with sticky or stinging cells which allow them to trap small prey.

1 Moon jellyfish
Aurelia aurita
Almost transparent. Contact with the tentacles produces a temporary sting. (15 in.)

2 Comb jellies
Mnemiopsis spp.
Rare, but may occur in great concentrations that blur underwater vision on some summer days. Harmless. (4 in.)

3 Portuguese man-of-war
Physalia physalis
Oceanic. Strong winds may blow them toward the shore. Toxins from the tentacles are extremely potent. If stung, the injured area should be treated with alcohol, diluted ammonia or meat tenderiser. Avoid rubbing with sand; remove any tentacles stuck to the skin one by one. (float: 6 in.; tentacles: 60 ft!)

4 Upsidedown jellyfish
Cassiopeia xamachana
Rare in reefs, but may cover the bottom in calm waters near mangroves. Tentacles have a weak toxin. (12 in.)

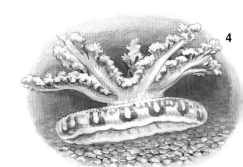

WORMS

Their lifestyles bear no resemblance to that of earthworms. Some roam the surface of the reef in search of food while others spend their entire lives encased in tubes of their own production.

5 Feather-duster worm
Sabellastarte magnifica
Inhabits flexible tubes which protrude from the sand. (crown diam.: 4 in.; body length: 5 in.)

6 Bristle worm
Hermodice carunculata
Feeds on coral polyps, gorgonians, anemones or black coral, preferring the early morning or dusk. The thin bristles on the sides are filled with toxin; on contact they produce considerable pain. (12 in.)

7 Christmas tree worm
Spirobranchus giganteus
When disturbed it quickly hides the colourful crest. Common on the surface of live coral. Feeds on plankton. (crown diam.: 1 in.; body length: 5 in.)

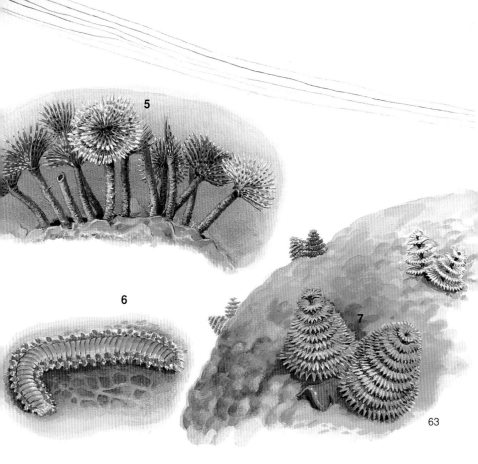

MOLLUSCS

Masters of architecture and armour, they are slaves of their weight, which makes them sluggish. Some live anchored to the substrate. Mostly nocturnal, they are timid as well; at the merest sign of danger they curl their bodies deep into the shell, or shut their valves, and remain so for many minutes. Molluscs are generally herbivores; they mow delicately-shaped algae, or filter plankton cells from the water using their gills as a net.

The largest and most exuberant Caribbean shells are rare today, and thus should not be collected.

1 Queen helmet
Cassis madagascarensis
The name *madagascarensis* is a misnomer, since the species only inhabits the Antilles. (14 in.)

2 King helmet
Cassis tuberosa
The lower 'walking' surface forms a nearly perfect triangle. Lives on sandy bottoms, where it feeds on sea urchins. (9 in.)

3 Flame helmet
Cassis flammea (5 in.)

4 Trumpet triton
Charonia variegata
Strictly nocturnal. Spends the daytime hidden in deep narrow crevices. Feeds on starfish and sea cucumbers. (14 in.)

5 Queen conch
Strombus gigas
The most common Caribbean sea shell. Lives on seagrass beds, where it feeds on microscopic algae. (12 in.)

6 Atlantic thorny oyster
Spondylus americanus
Generally dusted by sediment and covered by algae, sponges and other invertebrates. Not rare on deeper walls, but very hard to spot. (4 in.)

7 Atlantic wing oyster
Pteria colymbus
Most frequently found cohabiting with live gorgonians. (3 in.)

8 Reef squid
Sepiotheutis sepioidea
Lives at shallow depths, either alone or in groups of up to 20. Nocturnal; feeds on fishes. (10 in.)

9 Flamingo tongue
Cyphoma gibbosum
Common at shallow depths, always on gorgonians: feeding on their polyps. (1 in.)

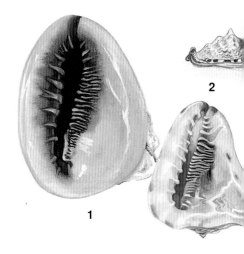

2

1

SHRIMPS, CRABS AND HERMIT CRABS

Crustacean armour is of a medieval nature; at times decorated as if for a carnival. Except for the smallest species, or the larvae, they are compelled to live on the bottom by the weight of their shells. All feed nocturnally, except those which live under the protection of stinging life forms or provide 'services' to potential predators. This lifestyle is mandatory, since many diurnal fishes have excellent vision and powerful jaws.

1 Spiny lobster
Panulirus argus
Common. Seen hiding by day in crevices, from where the antennae jut out. At night it moves in search of small molluscs and other bottom-dwelling invertebrates. (2 ft.)

2 Spotted spiny lobster
Panulirus guttatus
More abundant than commonly thought. Hides deep within dark crevices, which makes it difficult to spot. (8 in.)

3 Spanish lobster
Scyllarides aequinoctialis
Rare, most commonly observed during night dives. (1 ft.)

4 Conch hermit crab
Petrochirus diogenes
Very large. Adults need the empty Queen conch shell for shelter. Lives on muddy or sandy bottoms. (1 ft.)

5 Red hermit crab
Paguristes cadenati
Common, though seldom seen by day. (1 in.)

6

7

8

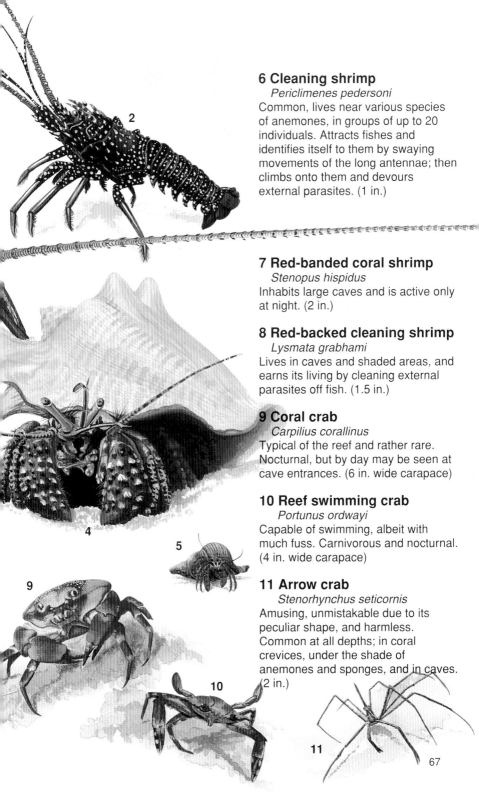

6 Cleaning shrimp
Periclimenes pedersoni
Common, lives near various species of anemones, in groups of up to 20 individuals. Attracts fishes and identifies itself to them by swaying movements of the long antennae; then climbs onto them and devours external parasites. (1 in.)

7 Red-banded coral shrimp
Stenopus hispidus
Inhabits large caves and is active only at night. (2 in.)

8 Red-backed cleaning shrimp
Lysmata grabhami
Lives in caves and shaded areas, and earns its living by cleaning external parasites off fish. (1.5 in.)

9 Coral crab
Carpilius corallinus
Typical of the reef and rather rare. Nocturnal, but by day may be seen at cave entrances. (6 in. wide carapace)

10 Reef swimming crab
Portunus ordwayi
Capable of swimming, albeit with much fuss. Carnivorous and nocturnal. (4 in. wide carapace)

11 Arrow crab
Stenorhynchus seticornis
Amusing, unmistakable due to its peculiar shape, and harmless. Common at all depths; in coral crevices, under the shade of anemones and sponges, and in caves. (2 in.)

SEA URCHINS, STARFISHES AND SEA CUCUMBERS

Living fortresses, the echinoderms appear to be ardently fond of geometry, mathematics and hydraulic engineering.

They may be shaped like a globe or a flat dish and covered with spines (sea urchins); comprised of several thicker or thinner fingers (starfishes); with small bodies from which protrude thin fingers which may or not subdivide to form a net (brittlestars and Basket starfish); like a duster (sea lilies); or cucumber-shaped (sea cucumbers).

The group as a whole is characterised by a body symmetry based on the number five or its multiples. Most species are capable of moving slowly over the bottom thanks to thousands of tiny feet that function by hydraulic pressure transmitted through a web of thin tubes.

1 Crinoids
Nemaster spp.
Born over 350 millions of years ago and abundant in the simpler oceans of that time, miraculously they survive in today's complex reefs. They come in various colours, and with 10, 20 and sometimes up to 40 arms. (15 in. diameter).

2 Brittlestars
(various genera: see illustration)
No less than 20 species are common in the Caribbean. They appear under every rock, within every sponge, or roaming the bottom. All feed on small animals, particularly at night. (6 in. max. diam.)

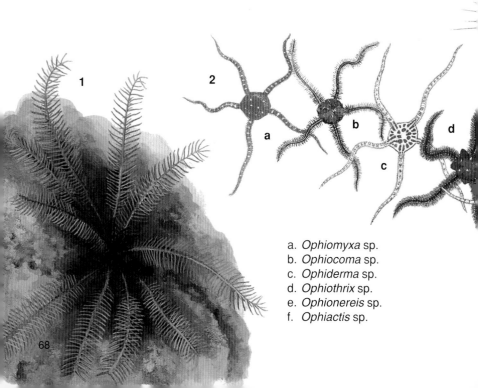

a. *Ophiomyxa* sp.
b. *Ophiocoma* sp.
c. *Ophiderma* sp.
d. *Ophiothrix* sp.
e. *Ophionereis* sp.
f. *Ophiactis* sp.

3 Long-spined urchin
Diadema antillarum
A truly untouchable animal; terrible and also admirable. The spines are hollow, venom-filled, brittle, and pierce the skin easily, producing a mild pain. (15 in., spines included)

4 Sea egg
Tripneustes ventricosus
Spines are somewhat blunt. Common at shallow depths, often using shells or seagrass blades as sunshades. (6 in.)

5 Slate-pencil urchin
Eucidaris tribuloides
Common between 20 and 80 feet. Spines are sometimes covered with algae. (2 in.)

6 Two-spined starfish
Astropecten duplicatus
Typically found buried in the sand in search of small molluscs. The spiny edges are dull and harmless. (6 in.)

7 Furry sea cucumber
Astichopus multifidus
Common on sandy patches of the reef. Ingests sand in order to digest the organic matter it contains. (18 in.)

8 Cushion star
Oreaster reticulatus
Formerly abundant on sandy or seagrass bottoms, particularly on very shallow water; now rare due to intense collecting. Carnivorous. (20 in.)

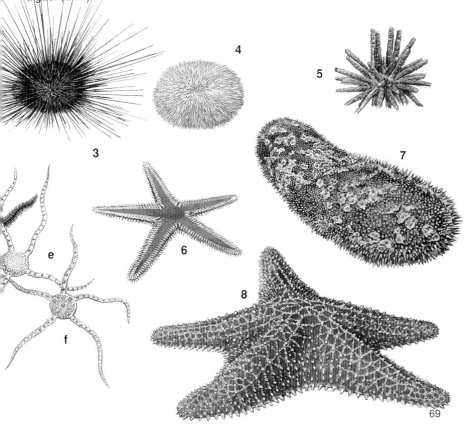

69

SEA TURTLES

Five species of great size inhabit the Western Atlantic, and are among the most valuable and esoteric reptiles on the planet. They are capable of swimming at considerable speed, of migrating thousands of miles through open seas, and of taking naps 200 feet below the surface. Their whole life is spent in the water; only adult females go ashore to dig into the sand at night and lay broods of up to 200 spherical eggs. Some two months later the newborn turtles scrape their way back to light and reach the ocean, totally unassisted by their parents.

Most turtle populations are in need of protection and in danger of extinction; man, who hunts them for their shell, amongst other things, is responsible.

1 Loggerhead turtle
Caretta caretta
Has a large head and very powerful jaws, capable of crushing an adult Queen conch shell. Migrates throughout the Antilles and Central America, but spawns mainly in temperate latitudes. (4.5 ft.)

2 Kemp's ridley turtle
Lepidochelys kempi
Rare outside the Gulf of Mexico. The entire population nests massively and at the same time on a single beach in the state of Tamaulipas, Mexico. Carnivorous. (3 ft.)

3 Leatherback turtle
Dermochelys coriacea
The largest of all living turtles, inhabits the open oceans. Extremely rare and of largely unknown habits. Devours great quantities of jellyfish. (7 ft.)

4 Green turtle
Chelonia mydas
Very common five centuries ago, but now almost extinct. Feeds on the abundant seagrass which grows on shallow bottoms. The shell of young specimens closely resembles that of the Hawksbill. (5 ft.)

5 Hawksbill turtle
Eretmochelys imbricata
Typical of coral reefs and very hard to spot when lying motionless among the corals. Feeds primarily on sponges. Produces the famous spotted shell greatly coveted by artisans. (3.5 ft.)

MARINE PLANTS

If judged by the impact on our senses, the reefs' opulence is animal rather than vegetable. But the reef area not occupied by corals or sand is entirely covered by various species of algae. Most are small, and are kept short due to the constant siege of herbivorous fishes and crabs. Lacking roots, trunk, leaves and flowers, they are simple and delicate. They are classified as green, brown or red, depending on whether they contain only green pigments (chlorophyll), or additional brown (fucoxanthin) or red (phycoerythrin) pigments.

Sea grasses are higher plants, sometimes very abundant in areas surrounding the reefs, and form the base of a very productive ecosystem. A multitude of algae thrive on the surface of the blades, under which hide many minute animal forms.

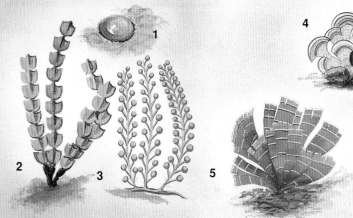

GREEN ALGAE

1 *Valonia* spp.
Lives at shallow depths, in coral crevices. (2 in. diam.)

2 *Halimeda* spp.
Hard to the touch due to extreme calcification. They are abundant and contribute to formation of sand. (10–25 in. wide)

3 *Caulerpa* spp.
Nearly 20 species exist in the region. All have a dragging stolon, with rising branches. (4–12 in.)

BROWN ALGAE

4 *Padina* spp.
Like a tree trunk, has semicircular lines that mark periods of quicker or slower growth. (6 in.)

5 *Stypopodium zonale*
Emits blue-green iridescence. Found from the coast to depths in excess of 100 feet. (15 in.)

6 *Dictyota* spp.
Can be abundant. Always flat and with a dichotomic branching. (10 in.)

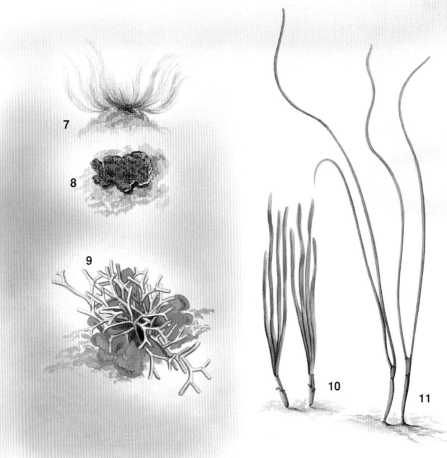

RED ALGAE

Comprises a complex group of species, all small. Thread-like and delicate, or calcareous, they grow in articulated fashion, like hard patches over the reef rock, or even like free rocky nodules.

7 Thread-like, not calcareous (8 in.)

8 Articulated, calcareous (6 in.)

9 Patch-like, calcareous (4 in.)

SEA GRASSES

10 Turtle grass
Thalassia testudinum
Very common in shallow water; grows thickly in extensive fields. The staple food of the Green turtle. (1 ft.)

11 Manatee grass
Cymodocea filiforme
The food of manatees, some fishes and the Queen conch. (20 in.)

THE REEF AT NIGHT

Night diving is not as dangerous as it seems, particularly if performed with SCUBA gear. Phosphorescent planktonic species are sometimes abundant and transmute divers into heavenly fairies.

The reef changes appearance at night. From the deeper crevices a new crowd of hustlers pour like magic; one outfitted to live in the dark, others with predominating reds and pinks, thick spiny armour, long antennae or bulging eyes. Meanwhile corals become completely covered with translucent, honey-coloured tentacles.

The numerous schools of fish have disappeared; many perhaps seek nourishment in far-away grass fields. Others of their lineage, like butterflyfish and parrotfish, have taken cover to rest. Cardinalfishes, porcupinefishes and burrfishes, on the contrary, emerge from the darkness of daytime clandestinity to full star- or moonlight, in search of plankton, molluscs, hermit crabs.

1 Reef octopus
Octopus briareus
Solitary. Always moves hugging the bottom in search of crustaceans and molluscs. Capable of changing colour and pattern in a second or two. Lives only one year. (2 ft. overall diam.)

2 Red coral shrimp
Rhynchocinetes rigens
Hides during the day in the deepest coral crevices. (2 in.)

3 Pearlfish
Carapus bermudensis
Strictly nocturnal, spends the day hidden inside the body of various species of sea cucumbers. Carnivorous. (8 in.)

4 Basket starfish
Astrophyton muricatum
Curls up and hides during daylight hours, but at dusk opens its arms to form a net, in which small drifting animals are trapped. (3 ft. diam.)

5 Heart urchin
Meoma ventricosa
Common. Buries itself in the sand during the day. Feeds on organic matter contained in sediments. One of the slowest animals in the world, advancing just a few inches per hour. (7 in.)

6 Spiny spider crab
Mithrax spinossisimus
The largest crab in the Caribbean region. Can weigh up to 5 lbs. (7 in. wide carapace)

2

The following species of cardinalfishes, and another 20 which inhabit the Antilles, feed on animal plankton and hunt only at night. Males incubate eggs in their mouths. During the day they hide among corals, under rocks, next to anemones, or in the mantle cavity of the Queen conch.

7 Freckled cardinalfish
Phaeoptyx conklini (2.5 in.)

8 Flamefish
Apogon maculatus (4.5 in.)

9 Barred cardinalfish
Apogon binotatus (3 in.)

REEF ETHICS

- Stony corals, sponges, and most other invertebrates are very delicate; the slightest contact with our hands, more so with diving fins, will damage the polyps or their tissues, and this may ease the way for pathogenic infections. Swim a few yards above the reef. To make long observations always rest on a patch of sand or on bare rock.
- Each anchor destroys several coral colonies; many anchors destroy whole reefs. Always drop yours on nearby large sandy areas.
- The best way to *use* a reef is to give it full protection. It will then be available for thousands of other people. Fishing and collecting – even empty shells – will alter delicate interrelationships, diminish diversity and beauty and generate subsequent damage.
- Avoid feeding the fish; this distortion of the normal balance of life could turn fish into beggars dependent on our favours.
- Coral reefs are unique environments, their inhabitants and happenings are capable of generating strong feelings, of changing our view of life, of turning us into better people. *That* is the major treasure. Leave behind among its creatures only the memory of the visit of peaceful and careful phantoms.

INDEX